THE TRUMP ADMINISTRATION

AND OTHER JOKES

The Trump Administration
and Other Jokes

Marc Brel

ShoreView Press

The Trump Administration and Other Jokes

Copyright 2017

by Marc Brel

ADVANCE PRAISE FOR *THE TRUMP ADMINISTRATION AND OTHER JOKES*:

"This is a really great book, I can tell you that. Really, really great, okay? It's even better than *The Art of the Deal.* You're going to laugh so much, you're going to be sick and tired of laughing. Believe me."

--"Donald Trump"

"Theese eez very fahnny boook. I leff so hard I puke. Even weethout poot feenger down throat, like usual. And pliz dun tell me Meechelle say same zing."

--Melania Trahmp

"Sure, it's a funny book, but it's supposed to be funny, it's a joke book. But I'll tell what's really a *joke* -- that they haven't thrown the *book* at Hillary Clinton for all her deceptions and emails and the Clinton Foundation and what about Benghazi? Why aren't you talking about that? She should have been *booked* for all the things she's done, and that's not *funny*. This books has laughs, but we have alternative laughs.

--Kellyanne Conjob

"Birth control makes women unattractive and crazy. Paul Ryan was grown in a petri dish. Would you rather your child had feminism or cancer? I want to bring everything crashing down."

--Steve Bannon

"This is humor in a splenic vein. Take it with you when you flee the country."

--R.U. Schittenme, author of *Get Out Now! How Trump Made America Emigrate Again*

To all those who didn't vote in the 2016 election,

without whom this would not have been possible

FOREWORD

By "Donald Trump"

I didn't really write this Foreword, okay? Saying I wrote it is just another example of how the dishonest, lying scum media works.

Sad!

Of course, I didn't write *The Art of the Deal*, either, but give me a break. Writing a book turns out to be really complicated. Nobody knew it was so complicated.

I have never written a Foreword. If I did, it would be much better than this one, right? It would be the best Foreword. It would be so good that the book would sell millions and millions of copies just because it had such a good Foreword. I'm going to write a Backward someday. When I do, it will be the best Backward, I can tell you that.

I didn't even read this book, okay? The last time I read a book was never. And I for sure didn't write that blurb up there saying this book was better than *The Art of the Deal*, which was totally the best book ever, right? Even better than the Bible. When I said the Bible was better, I was just being nice. I am so, so yuugely nice, okay? Everybody says so. There's a lot of really stupid stuff in the Bible. Thou shalt not commit adultery, who said that? What a loser. I committed adultery, and bragged about it in the *Post*, and I'm President and He's not. And that stuff about it's easier for a camel to go through the eye of a needle than for a rich guy to get into heaven? Give me a break. Total garbage. I'm going to sue whoever said that and gets lots and lots of money.

I was going to sue whoever put my name on this Foreword and that blurb until I realized that they put quotation marks around my name, so it's okay. Like when I said that Obama "wire tapped" me. I put quotation marks around wire tapped, see? So it could mean something other than wire tapped, and somebody other than Obama, and somebody other than me, right? I have a very good brain, I can tell you that.

Go ahead and read this book if you want. It's a free country. For now.

We'll see, okay?

CONTENTS

*"The trouble with practical jokes
is that very often they get elected."*

--Will Rogers

1

THE TRUMP ADMINISTRATION AND SIXTY MORE
TRUMP JOKES

THE TRUMP ADMINISTRATION is running the country like a business. Unfortunately, the business is Trump University.

*****

Trump goes to one of Washington D.C.'s high-end brothels. He tells the madam that he has a unique request.

"I can assure you that whatever you are looking for, we can accommodate you," says the madam. "What is it you want?"

Trump says, "I want someone who will do it the Trump Way."

"I will give you our most versatile girl," says the madam. "She can handle anything. I will take you to her room."

When he meets the girl, Trump says, "Are you ready to do it the Trump Way?"

"Sure," she says. "Let's go."

They have sex, then Trump gets up, puts on his clothes, and starts to leave.

"Hey, wait a minute," says the prostitute. "You didn't pay me."

Trump says, "Of course I didn't pay you. That's the Trump Way."

*****

The Justice Department held hearings to investigate Russian interference in the election. Attorney General Jeff Sessions chaired the hearings.

Retired General and former National Security Advisor Michael Flynn was called to testify. A Justice Department prosecutor opened the questioning.

"Isn't it true that you accepted payments from Russian agents to interfere with this investigation?"

General Flynn stared off into the distance, as if he had not heard the question. The prosecutor asked again, "Is it not true, sir, that you accepted large amounts of money from agents of the Russian government to interfere with this investigation?"

Again, the witness did not respond. Finally, Jeff Sessions said, "Please answer the question, General Flynn."

Flynn looked startled. "Oh," he said. "I thought he was talking to you."

*****

President Trump visits a primary school for a photo op, and to speak to the children about his great victory in the election. After his speech, he offers to take questions from the children.

A second grader raises his hand, and the president asks him what his name is.

"My name is Zachary."

"Nice name. Very good name. Not a great name, but an okay name. I love the Jewish people."

"I'm not Jewish."

"What's your question, Zach?"

"I have three questions. First, why do you think the crowd at your inauguration was so much smaller than the crowd at President Obama's inauguration? Second, how many members of your campaign staff had contact with Russian agents during the campaign? And third, how many people will lose health insurance coverage under your plan?"

The bell rings for recess. President Trump says that he will continue after the recess.

When the children get back, President Trump says, "Now where was I? I think it was question and answer time, right? I have such a great memory, I can tell you that. Any of you have a question?"

A different boy raises his hand. President Trump asks him what his name is.

"David."

"What's your question, Dave?"

David says, "I have five questions. First, why do you think the crowd at your inauguration was so much smaller than the crowd at President Obama's inauguration? Second, how many members of your campaign staff had contact with Russian agents during the campaign? Third, how many people will lose health insurance coverage under your plan? Fourth, why did the bell for recess go off 15 minutes early? And fifth, what happened to Zachary?"

*****

A month after Donald and Melania were first married, one of Melania's fashion model friends noticed that Melania looked sad, and asked her if anything was wrong.

"Yes, sahmzing is naught right."

"What is it?" said her friend.

"Eet eez our sex life," said Melania.

"What's wrong with your sex life?"

"All he does," says Melania, "is stend by bed and tell me how great eez going to be."

*****

Q: When Donald Trump has a woman up to his hotel room, and he wants to set the mood, why does he always put on a recording of *Clare de Lune*?

A: Because he likes to grab them by Debussy.

President Trump and Secretary of State Rex Tillerson flew to Baghdad on an important diplomatic mission. On the flight over, Trump regaled Tillerson and the accompanying Secret Service agents with his usual patter about his great victory in the 2016 election.

Air Force One landed at the airport in Baghdad, and Trump, Tillerson, and the Secret Service agents disembarked. Tillerson was surprised to see that they were only greeted by a small group of rather nervous-looking Iraqi diplomats, accompanied by airport security personnel.

Tillerson said to Trump, "I was expecting to see some American military here to provide security, Mr. President. Where are our soldiers?"

"We outsource military security in Baghdad, Rex," said Trump. "My son-in-law Jared is in charge of arranging that. We have a contract with Blackwater."

"Blackwater?" said Tillerson. "We used them during the Iraq war. They caused a lot of trouble. Why are we still using them?"

Trump said, "I made a great deal. We use Blackwater for military security, they use Trump hotels wherever they go. I scratch their back, they scratch mine. That's how government works, Rex, now that we're running government like a business. Besides, Rex, you know my Secretary of Education, Betsy? Her brother owns Blackwater. That's how government works, now."

"What about Iraqi military?" said the Secretary.

"I don't know," said Trump. "I'd ask them about that, but I don't speak Iraqi. Do you speak Iraqi?"

"There is no such language as Iraqi. They speak Arabic."

"That's amazing you know that. Nobody knows that. That's why I named you Secretary of State."

Just then, a caravan of black SUVs came streaming across the tarmac at them. The SUVs screeched to a halt, and black-clad ISIS fighters armed with assault rifles jumped out. The airport security personnel scattered. The ISIS fighters greatly outnumbered the Secret Service agents, and after a brief firefight, Trump and Tillerson were taken hostage. They were bound and shoved into the back of one of the SUVs, which sped away from the airport, across the desert.

Bouncing along in the back of the SUV, Trump said to Tillerson, "I just know that somehow, this is Obama's fault. It's happening because the Democrats can't get over how badly they lost. It was the greatest election upset of all time."

The SUV pulled up to the nearest ISIS headquarters, where Trump and Tillerson were hauled into a stone building, and brought before an ISIS commander.

"Allah be praised!" said the commander. "We have captured the American president and secretary of state. This is a great victory for the Islamic State and for all the people!"

Trump said to the commander, "I bet you guys are planning to get some yuuuge ransom for us. Lots and lots of money."

"You might think so, but you would be wrong," said the commander. "I just got off the phone with al Baghdadi. He made an attempt to present our demands to your vice president Pence, but Pence would not take the call. Everybody knows there's no way we are letting you go. We are going to behead you, how could we not? Everybody knows we are going to behead you. So no one is interested in paying any ransom. By the way, we could not believe how easy it was to capture you. It is almost as if whoever was in charge of arranging your security had no experience whatsoever in military or antiterrorist activities. On top of that, paying off your private security firm was child's play. They act just like a business for profit, not like the army of a great nation."

"Sad!" said Trump.

"But because you are leaders of a nation," said the commander, "and to show you that we are not the barbarians you make us out to be, before you are beheaded, we will grant you each one last request."

The commander walked up to Trump. "Have you a last request, before you die?"

"Yes," said Trump. "Before I die, I would like to tell you guys all about my great victory in the 2016 presidential election. They said that there was no way I could get to 270 electoral college votes, but I got to 304. It was the biggest landslide of all time. I ran an absolutely great campaign. No one could believe how great it was. I just want to tell you all about it."

"Very well," said the commander. "You will be allowed to tell us about your campaign and the election, in as much detail as you wish. Then, you shall be beheaded."

The commander walked up to Tillerson. "Have you a last request?"

"Yes," said Tillerson.

"What is your request?"

"*Please*," said Tillerson. "Cut my head off *before* Trump tells his story."

*****

Q: Why is *The Art of the Deal* like one of Trump's actual businesses?

A: They both have a Chapter 11.

*****

Trump: "Vladimir, it's Donald calling. I wanted to offer my personal condolences on the accidental death of that very famous Russian dissident poet I heard about."

Putin: "Shhhhh. Accidental death of Russian dissident poet is *next* week."

*****

A high school social studies teacher decided to test her students' knowledge of famous presidential quotations.

"Who said, 'We have nothing to fear but fear itself?'"

Only one student in the class, a recent immigrant from Mexico named Maria, raised her hand. The teacher called on her.

"Franklin Roosevelt," said Maria.

"That's right," said the teacher. "Very good. Now, who said 'Ask not what your country can do for you. Ask what you can do for your country?'"

Again, only Maria raised her hand, and the teacher called on her.

"John Kennedy," said Maria.

"Correct," said the teacher. "That's very good, but it bothers me a little that the only student in this class who knows these famous presidential quotations is a girl who moved to this country very recently from Mexico."

A voice from the back of the classroom said, "Fuck Mexican immigrants!"

The teacher was startled. "Who said that?"

Maria said, "Donald Trump."

*****

Q: What's the difference between a garbanzo bean and a chickpea?

A: Donald Trump has never had a garbanzo bean on his face.

*****

A clown, a con man and a sexual predator walk into a bar.

The bartender says, "Hello, Mr. President."

*****

President Trump invited John McCain to lunch at the White House, to try to hash out some of their political differences.

After about 5 minutes, McCain suddenly stood up, and said, "I've had enough. You're lying!"

"Of course I'm lying," said Trump. "But hear me out..."

*****

President Trump's son-in-law, Jared Kushner, is in an automobile accident, and is taken to the hospital. He is unconscious for three days. When he comes to, he finds Ivanka sitting next to his hospital bed.

26

"What happened?" says Jared.

"You were in a terrible accident," says Ivanka. "You have been unconscious for three days."

"Three days?" says Jared. "How long have you been here?"

"I have been here at your bedside the whole time, darling."

"Oh my God," says Jared. "If I have been unconscious for three days, and you have been here the whole time, who's running the country?"

*****

President Trump has a female White House intern alone in the Oval Office, and decides to have a little fun with her.

"You know," says Trump, "Hillary never had a chance against me. You know why? I'll tell you why. Because for all the fuss made by the feminists over the past 30 years, Washington is still a man's world. Always has been, believe me. I mean, just look at the Washington Monument. It's obviously a phallic symbol, okay? Don't you think the Washington Monument is a phallic symbol?"

"What's a phallic symbol?" says the intern.

"It's something that represents, or looks like, a phallus," says Trump.

"What's a phallus?" says the intern.

Trump smiles, stands up and walks out from behind his desk. He opens his belt and fly, unbuttons his pants, and drops his pants and briefs.

"There," says Trump. "That's a phallus."

"Oh, I see," says the intern. "It's like a prick, only smaller."

*****

Jimmy Carter dies and goes to heaven. St. Peter greets him in the presidential greeting room of heaven. Carter notices that there are many clocks on the wall, and asks St. Peter about them.

"Those are the presidential lie clocks," says St. Peter. "Every time a president lies, the hands on his clock move. That's how we here in heaven keep track of how honest a president is."

Carter points to one of the clocks. "I see that the hands on this clock have not moved at all. Is it broken?"

"Nothing in heaven is broken," says St. Peter. "That's George Washington's clock. He never told a lie, so the hands never moved."

"The hands on this clock have only moved a little. Whose clock is that?"

"That's Abraham Lincoln's clock. He only lied a few times. The clock directly beneath it is your clock. It moved a few more times than Lincoln's. The clock to the left of yours is Nixon's. You can see the hands of that clock moved a lot."

Carter looks around. "Where is Donald Trump's clock?"

St. Peter says, "It's in Jesus's office. He's using it as a ceiling fan."

*****

Trump is worried about the future of his administration, so he goes to see a fortuneteller recommended to him by his chief strategist, Steve Bannon. The fortuneteller reads Trump's palm, which, owing to the size of his hands, is a quick read. The fortuneteller looks up.

"I see," says the fortuneteller, "that you will die."

"I will die?" says Trump. "That's a disaster. A total disaster. Are you sure this isn't fake fortune-telling? I'm the healthiest president ever, okay? My doctor says so. Everybody says so."

"Nevertheless, I see that you will die."

"When will I die?"

"You will die," says the fortuneteller, "on a Mexican holiday."

"A Mexican holiday?" says Trump. "Which Mexican holiday?"

The fortuneteller says, "Any day you die will be a Mexican holiday."

*****

Trump's son, Barron, is sent home from school one day with a note from his teacher. He shows it to his mother.

"I dun know what is thees meaning," says Melania. "Show to father."

Barron goes to Trump's study, where Trump is busy tweeting about how pathetic Arnold Schwarzenegger is. Barron walks over to Trump's desk.

"I'm very busy right now," says Trump. "What is it, Byron?"

"My name is Barron."

"That's what I said. I totally said Barron, I can tell you that. Don't believe the lying media reports that I don't know my son's name, okay? They're total scum. So what's the problem?"

"My teacher sent me home with a note for you," says Barron. He hands Trump the note.

The note says: "Today in class I asked Barron who killed Martin Luther King. He said, 'I didn't do it.' Given your position, I thought you should know about this."

Trump reads the note slowly, and nods his head thoughtfully. He looks at Barron.

"So tell me, son," says Trump. "Didja' do it?"

*****

Trump and Bannon die and go to heaven. When they get there, they are surprised to see that there are ducks everywhere. Thousands of ducks, all around them.

St. Peter appears, and says, "We only have one rule here in heaven. Do not step on a duck. Enjoy eternity however you want, but don't step on a duck."

Two weeks later, Bannon accidentally steps on a duck. St. Peter appears, accompanied by an extremely unattractive, unpleasant woman. She is loud, vulgar and gross-looking.

St. Peter says, "Bannon, you stepped on a duck. You were warned not to do that. As a consequence, you will spend the rest of eternity in the company of this woman."

St. Peter shackles Bannon to the woman and disappears. Bannon walks away, forlornly.

Wow, thinks Trump. I wouldn't want to be in his shoes. I'm going to be really careful not to step on a duck.

A whole year goes by, and Trump is enjoying himself, although walking very carefully. All of a sudden St. Peter appears, accompanied this time by an absolutely beautiful woman. She's a ten, thinks Trump. In addition, the woman appears to have a delightful, pleasant way about her.

"This is your companion for all eternity," says St. Peter.

He shackles Trump to the woman, and disappears. Trump is ecstatic.

"This is wonderful," says Trump. "I wonder what I did to deserve to spend eternity with someone like you."

"I don't know about you," says the woman, "but I stepped on a duck."

*****

Steve Bannon went to a doctor.

"What brings you here today?" said the doctor.

"Yesterday I took a good look at myself in a mirror," said Bannon. "I was shocked. My face is all puffy and misshapen, my skin is blotchy, with red patches all over my nose and cheeks, my eyes are bloodshot, with puffy, dark bags under them, my teeth are dingy, and my mouth is twisted in an ugly scowl. I look horrible. Is something wrong with me?"

"Well, one thing I can tell you," said the doctor. "There's nothing wrong with your eyesight."

*****

Q: How many Trump White House staffers does it take to change a lightbulb?

A: The lightbulb needs to change, I can tell you that. People are saying the lightbulb is burned out. It's a

32

disaster. A total disaster, believe me. It's a mess. I inherited a mess, and a burned-out lightbulb. It burned out because of Obama's weak policies and Susan Rice trying to put too much light on things. But it's going to change, okay? It's got to change, so we're going to change it. I'm not going to tell you what I'm going to do about it or when, I'm going to keep you guessing, but it's going to change, I can tell you that. It's going to change, *bigly*.

*****

Melania: "Today Vite House ductor give me feezeecul exam."

Donald: "What did he say?"

Melania: "He say I very feet. He ulso say I have bootiful breasts."

Trump: "That pisses me off. Did he say anything about your fat ass?"

Melania: "Yes. He say you should lose sahm vate."

*****

Q: What's really long and hangs in front of an asshole?

A: Trump's necktie.

*****

Donald and Melania Trump are invited to a party at Bill and Hillary Clinton's house. In an attempt to show goodwill toward his former opponent, Trump accepts the invitation. At the party, he comments on the Clinton's home to Melania.

"This place is a dump," says Trump. "A total dump. Our place at Trump Tower is much better, right? So is our place at Mar-a-Lago. All of our places are much better than this place. It's not even very big. It's the kind of place losers live. It's a disaster."

"There must be samzink you are likink about it," says Melania.

"Well," says Trump. "I kind of like the solid gold urinal. That's pretty cool."

As the Trumps are leaving the party, Bill and Hillary come to the door to say goodbye to them. Melania realizes that proper etiquette calls for her to say something nice to Hillary about her home.

"Heelary," she says. "Doanald vas very much eempressed weeth your solid gold urinal."

Hillary turns to Bill and says, "I just figured out who pissed in your saxophone."

*****

Trump walks into the bar at Mar-a-Lago, where he is well known by all. As he is sitting down at one end of the bar, a patron at the other end of the bar yells out, "Hey, bartender! Get a drink on me for that douchebag who just walked in!"

As the bartender is profusely apologizing to Trump, the man at the other end of the bar again yells out, "Bartender! I said get a drink on me for that douchebag!"

The bartender signals the bouncer to come over and remove the offensive patron from the premises. He says to Trump, "I am very sorry for that person's rude behavior, sir. Of course, anything for you is on the house. What will you have?"

Trump says, "I'll have my usual. Vinegar and water."

*****

One morning at Mar-a-Lago, President Trump realizes that one of the downsides to being president is that he doesn't get to drive anymore. He tells his Secret Service detail that he wants to take the presidential limousine for a spin, and he doesn't want them to give him any trouble about it. He walks to his limousine, where he finds his chauffeur sitting in the back seat, taking a break, eating a sandwich.

"Just relax," says Trump, "I'm going to drive today. I miss driving. I'm a very good driver, I can tell you that. One of the best. Maybe the best driver you've ever seen. Maybe the best driver anybody's ever seen, okay? I'm going to get this baby out on Alligator Alley and really open 'er up."

Trump pulls the limousine onto the freeway, and starts

driving faster and faster. Eventually, a state trooper pulls the limousine over. The trooper walks up to the limo, and Trump rolls down the window, with a big smile on his face. The trooper looks inside the limo, and immediately walks back to his squad car.

The state trooper calls into headquarters and asks to speak to his captain.

"Captain," says the trooper, "I don't know what to do. I just pulled over the most important person in the world. The car was going over 100 miles per hour. What should I do?"

"The most important person in the world? Who the hell did you pull over?"

"I don't know, but he's sitting in the backseat of the limo, eating a sandwich, and Trump is his driver!"

*****

Q: Why is President Trump like a turtle sitting on top of a fence post?

A: You know he didn't get up there by himself, he doesn't belong up there, he doesn't know what to do up there, and you wonder what kind of an idiot put him there.

*****

Washington, D.C. got ten inches of fresh snow overnight,

and Trump stepped outside to see the beautiful white snow on the White House lawn. He was distressed to see that right in the middle of the lawn someone had written, "Trump sucks!" in urine.

He immediately got on the phone and called the head of the F.B.I., James Comey.

"I want an investigation of this outrage right away," said Trump.

"That is a disturbing security breach, sir," said Comey. "I'll get on it right away."

"Good. And by the way, thanks for sabotaging Clinton in the election by sending that message to Congress about the emails."

"Don't mention it," said Comey.

"I mean it," said Trump. "Thank you."

"I said DON'T MENTION IT!"

Three days later, Comey calls Trump and tells him that the investigation is completed.

"I'm afraid I have some bad news, sir," says Comey. "We did a DNA analysis of the urine, and it matched Bill Clinton's."

"That doesn't surprise me at all," said Trump. "I always knew Bill Clinton was a really bad, sick guy."

"That's not the bad news," said Comey.

"What's the bad news?"

"It's Melania's handwriting."

*****

Q: How does Donald Trump sleep?

A: First he lies on one side, then he lies on the other.

*****

Trump starts to worry one day that he isn't satisfying Melania in bed. He figures that his press secretary, Sean Spicer, can keep a secret, and that being a young, energetic guy, he might have some tips.

"It's not a problem with size," Trump tells Spicer, putting air quotes around "size." "There's no problem with that. Believe me. No problem at all, I can tell you that."

Spicer swallows several pieces of gum, and says, "I get it. I know when not to take you literally. So you mean it does have to do with size. But I don't know anything about this. You should ask a black guy about this. Supposedly they, you know, have big, well, hands and whatever. You have black friends, right?"

"Of course," says Trump. "I have lots of black friends. The blacks love me." Trump has to think for awhile about whether he knows any black guys. Then he gets an idea, and goes to Ben Carson's office, where Carson is asleep at his desk.

38

"Wake up, Ben," says Trump.

"What?" says Carson. "Whodat? Where's my luggage?"

Trump explains his problem to Carson, but since Ben is a doctor, Trump admits it might have something "to do with size.

Carson says, "I'm not an expert on that organ. I only know about the brain. I know everything about the brain. Did you know that if I put electrodes in your brain you would be able to remember every word of a book your mother read when you were in her uterus?"

Trump gives up and goes back to the Oval Office. He can't think of anyone else to talk to, until he remembers how well he got along with Kanye West. He gives Kanye a call, and explains his problem.

"I understand, Mr. President. I understand," says Kanye. "And I am honored you axed me about this. I tell you what I do. When I'm about to put it to my lady, after I'm sprung, I whacks it against the bedpost 'bout 10 times or so. Makes a difference."

Trump thanks him for the suggestion, and looks forward to his next trip to Trump Tower, since Melania never comes to the White House.

Trump arrives at Trump Tower late at night, and tiptoes into the pitch dark bedroom, where Melania is sleeping. He drops his pants, and starts whacking his dick against the bedpost.

Whump, whump, whump.

Melania suddenly sits bolt upright, and says, "Is that you,

Kanye?"

One day Donald Trump says to Melania, "I have some good news and some bad news."

"Vaht is good news?" says Melania.

"The good news," says Trump, "is that I got my immigration policy passed, and it's going to be implemented soon."

"That's mahvelous, dahlink," says Melania. "Vaht is bed news?"

"Barron is going to miss you."

Q: How can you tell when Donald Trump is lying?

A: His thumbs are moving.

The Chairman of the Joint Chiefs of Staff calls the Secretary of Defense to tell him that the nuclear launch codes need to be changed.

"We need to make them longer than 140 characters,"

says the Chairman.

"Why is it that?" says the Secretary.

"So Trump can't tweet them."

******

Donald and Melania Trump have Bill and Hillary Clinton over to their place at Trump Tower for a private dinner. After dinner, Bill Clinton says, "I have a wild idea. Just to show how well we all get along, and that there's no hard feelings and all that, why don't we try mate swapping?"

To Bill's surprise, the others all agree. They pair off and go to separate bedrooms.

Afterwards, Hillary lies in bed with a big smile on her face.

"Wow," she says. "That was amazing. That was by far the best sex I've ever had. I'd sure like to do it again sometime."

Then, she gets up onto one elbow and says, "I wonder how the boys are doing."

*****

Trump goes on a diplomatic tour of Africa. While he is visiting a small, obscure tribe in the interior of the continent, the ambassador informs him that the local chief, being quite honored by the visit, is giving Trump the companionship of the chief's most beautiful daughter for the night, as a gift. Trump says he is not interested in spending the night with the chief's daughter. The ambassador explains to Trump that, if he refuses the gift, the chief will be greatly offended. This, says the ambassador, could have an adverse effect on American relations with the entire region. Trump reluctantly agrees to have the chief's daughter in his room that night.

When she gets to Trump's room, the chief's daughter takes off all her clothes and gets into bed. Trump gets into the bed with her. When he approaches her, she gets up onto all fours, and offers herself doggy style. Trump has no experience with this position, and isn't sure he can do it, because of his small, um, shall we say, hands. He decides to mount her and do the best he can.

As soon as he starts, he hears the chief's daughter say, "Wunga bunga!"

Trump thinks, "She likes it, I must be pretty good at it this way. And why not? I'm really good at everything." He keeps going.

"Wunga bunga! Wunga bunga!" shouts the chief's daughter.

"Wow," thinks Trump. "I am so amazing." He finishes up.

"Wunga bunga," moans the chief's daughter.

The next day, Trump plays golf with the chief. On the first tee, the chief hits a perfect drive that lands on the green and rolls into the cup. Trump decides to show how smart he is by complimenting the chief in the chief's own language.

"Wunga bunga!" says Trump.

The chief turns and looks at Trump.

"What you mean," says the chief, "*wrong hole?*"

*****

Q: What does Kellyanne Conway call a telegram?

A: Alternative fax.

*****

Q: What does Sean Spicer call questions he's never heard before?

A: Alternative FAQs.

*****

Q: What does Donald Trump call bisexuals?

A: Alternative fags.

*****

Q: What does Donald Trump call his mistresses?

A: Alternative fucks.

*****

Q: What does Kellyanne Conway call Breitbart News?

A: Alternative Fox.

*****

Q: What's the difference between Kellyanne Conway and a rattlesnake?

A: The rattlesnake doesn't wear so much makeup.

*****

Q: What's the difference between Kellyanne Conway and an actress on Game of Thrones?

A: The Game of Thrones actress doesn't wear so much makeup.

*****

Q: Why did Donald Trump sign an Executive Order prohibiting the selling of pre-shredded cheese?

A: He wanted to make America grate again.

*****

Donald and Melania are attending a State banquet at the White House, standing in the reception line. Melania stands between her husband and the Secretary of State, Rex Tillerson. She tells Tillerson that she is a little nervous, because she does not recognize any of the guests.

"Don't worry," says Tillerson. "I'll whisper to you who each of the guests are before they get to you in the line. It will seem like you know everybody."

As the first guest approaches, Tillerson says, "That's Dmitry Rybolovlev. The Russian fertilizer king."

Melania offers her hand. "Pleased to meet you, Mr.Rybolovlev," she says.

Trump says, "Nice to see you, Dmitry."

The next guest approaches. Tillerson whispers to Melania, "That's Vladimir Potanin. He's the richest guy in Russia."

"How do you do, Mr. Potanin," says Melania.

"Howdy, Vlad," says Trump.

Another guest approaches. Tillerson says, "That's Leonid Mikhelson. He's owns the Russian gas company."

"Good evening, Mr. Mikhelson," says Melania.

"Hi, Leo," says Trump.

At this point, Melania turns to Donald and says, "Dahlink, when we have party, why eez eet always *your* friends?"

*****

A lot of people have been saying that Trump is like Hitler. This is ridiculous. Here are 10 ways in which Trump is not like Hitler:

1. Hitler actually wrote his own book.

2. Hitler didn't kowtow to the Russians.

3. Hitler was never divorced.

4. Hitler never made false claims that he was wiretapped.

5. Hitler didn't dye his face orange.

6. Hitler wasn't fat.

7. Hitler never talked about the size of his penis.

8. Hitler was a good public speaker.

9. Hitler paid the people who did work for him.

10. Okay, we could only come up with nine.

*****

Trump: "Would you like to have sex on my desk in the Oval Office?"

Melania: "Yes, of course, dahlink. Perhaps sahmtime when you are at Mar-a-Lago."

*****

Trump finds himself making an unusually large number of mental mistakes, even for him, and begins to worry that he isn't as sharp as he used to be. He remembers that his Secretary of Housing, Ben Carson, is an expert on the brain. He goes to Carson's office, where he finds Ben asleep at his desk.

"Wake up, Ben."

"Huh? Whazis? Who? Oh, my luggage!"

"It's me, Ben."

"Who?"

"The President."

Carson says nothing.

"Of the United States."

"Oh, yeah," says Carson. "I gotcha'. Boy, it's hard to adjust to that. What's hap'nin'?"

"Well, as you know, Ben, I have a very good brain. One

of the best. Maybe the best brain of anybody you'll ever know. Right?"

"Oh, for sure, Mr. President. Why, did you know that if I stuck electrodes into your brain you could remember every word of every book your father read before the sperm that made you was ejaculated into your mother?"

"That's amazing, Ben," says Trump. "So what I want will be easy for you."

"Whazzat?"

"Well, lately I seem to making a few mental mistakes, which is so totally unlike me. I mean, I never make mistakes and I'm never sorry about anything, but lately I've had a few, um..."

"Senior moments?"

"I don't know who that is, but he sounds Mexican. Do you have anthing that, you know, would make me, well..."

"Smarter?" says Carson.

"It would be for the good of the country," says Trump.

"Got just the thing right here," says Carson.

Carson opens a drawer in his desk, and takes out a bottle of pills. "These will make you much smarter, but unfortunately, they are very expensive. They cost $10,000 per pill."

"No problem," says Trump. "No problem at all. I have an excellent health insurance plan. Not a disaster like Obamacare. I'll take a gross of those pills, and charge it to my excellent government health care plan."

"They're not covered by insurance."

"Still no problem," says Trump. "The beautiful thing about me is, I'm very rich. Charge it to my personal account."

"Will do," says Carson.

Trump asks if he could try one of the pills right now. Carson opens the bottle, taps a pill into his palm and hands it to Trump. Trump pops it in his mouth.

"Hey!" says Trump. "This is nothing but a plain, ordinary TicTac. You son-of-a-bitch, you cheated me."

"You see," says Carson. "You're getting smarter already."

*****

Q: What do Donald Trump and Jared Kushner have in common?

A: They both want to bang Ivanka.

*****

The house staff at Trump Tower report that Melania screams during sex.

Especially when Donald walks in on her.

*****

Q: What do they call Trump's plane?

A: Hair Force One.

*****

Q: What does Melania see in Donald?

A: Billions of dollars and high cholesterol.

*****

Sean Spicer is hosting a new Sunday morning news show on television. It's called Beat the Press.

*****

Donald Trump attended an event hosted by the State Department honoring former secretaries of state. He found himself standing next to John Kerry, which, given some of the things he had said about Kerry, was very awkward. Trump did his best to make conversation.

"I don't get it," said Trump. "You're a rich guy, John. Your wife is a ketchup heiress. Heinz ketchup. That's the biggest ketchup there is. Yuuuge ketchup. Big, big money. Why are you such a dedicated, lifelong

Democrat?"

"Well," said Kerry, "my father was a Democrat, and my grandfather was a Democrat."

"That's your reason?" said Trump. "What if your father and grandfather had been couple of crooks?"

"You're right," said Kerry. "Then I would've been a Republican."

*****

The Trumps are flying over a poor neighborhood in New York.

Donald: "You know, I could just throw ten $100 bills out of the plane, and make ten people happy."

Melania: "Wery nice idea, dahlink. But for same price, you could throw tventy $50 beels out of plen, and make tventy pipple happy."

Barron: "But daddy, you could throw 100 ten dollar bills out of the plane, and make 100 people happy!"

Pilot (under breath): "Or, you could throw yourself out of the plane, and make millions of people happy."

*****

Q: What do you get when you cross a fraudster with a fashion model?

A: Barron.

*****

Donald Trump recently signed an Executive Order outlawing the use of cardboard and plastic shipping containers.

He wants to make America crate again.

*****

Q: What happens when Donald Trump takes Viagra?

A: He gets taller.

*****

Q: If Donald Trump and Steve Bannon were both on a ship that went down, who would be saved?

A: America.

*****

President Trump has gone on a fact-free diet.

Donald Trump goes to Ben Carson's office.

"Wake up, Ben," says Trump.

"Whozawassis?" says Carson.   "My luggage!   My luggage!"

"I need some advice," says Trump. "Little Marco's joke about my size is still getting a lot of mileage. There's no problem down there, believe me, but I see reports that people are still making jokes about it, okay?   Can you think of some way we can get these morons to knock it off?"

"Sure," says Carson. "Here's what to do. Sometimes a lot of members of the press hang out around the White House swimming pool. Next time they're down there, put on a pair of Speedo's, drop a potato in them, and go down for a dip in the pool."

"Great idea," says Trump. "I always knew you were a really smart guy."

The next day, Trump shows up in the doorway of Carson's office, in his Speedo's, dripping wet.

"Wake up, Ben!"

"What? Who? Luggage."

"Your idea didn't work at all," says Trump. "Those moron reporters just laughed at me."

"Next time," says Carson, "try putting the potato in front."

2

A COUPLE OF DOZEN TRUMP JOKES FROM THE
PROS

AND A HALF DOZEN FROM OTHER POLITICIANS

"Donald Trump had yet another awkward moment today. Apparently there was a crying baby at one of his rallies, and Trump actually kicked it out, saying, 'Get the baby out of here.' It backfired when the Secret Service tried to remove Trump."

--Jimmy Fallon

*****

"Donald Trump has come out in favor of shutting down Planned Parenthood. However, experts say, if he really wants Planned Parenthood to go under he should turn it into a Trump property."

-- Conan O'Brien

*****

"This guy has an ego. When Trump bangs a supermodel, he closes his eyes and imagines he's jerking off."

--Seth MacFarlane

*****

"Donald Trump, without a doubt, you're a New York landmark. Which means it will only be a matter of time before you bulldoze yourself and put up some gaudy, tacky monstrosity, and put your name on it."

-- Larry King

*****

"Donald, I'm not sure you're even aware of this, but the only difference between you and Michael Douglas from the movie, Wall Street, is that no one is going to be sad when you get cancer."

-- Anthony Jeselnik

*****

"I've heard word that Donald Trump has done so much damage to the New York skyline, that instead of calling him the Donald, they should call him the 20th hijacker."

-- Gilbert Gottfried

*****

"Is it possible that we've all been groped by Donald J. Trump, but just didn't feel it because of his tiny baby hands?"

-- Stephen Colbert

*****

"Trump's campaign manager, Kellyanne Conway, said this morning that Republicans should decide whether or not they support Donald Trump and 'stop pussyfooting around.' That's the worst choice of words since Abraham Lincoln said, 'I need slavery like I need a hole in the head.'"

-- Seth Meyers

*****

"If God gave comedians the power to invent people, the first person we would invent is Donald Trump."

-- Jerry Seinfeld

*****

"In an exclusive interview with the Christian Broadcasting Network, Donald Trump said, 'I believe in God.' But of course, The Donald was talking about himself."

-- Jay Leno

*****

"Donald Trump has canceled a planned trip to Israel. When asked why, Trump said, 'they already have a wall and a fear of Muslims. My work there is done.'"

-- Conan O'Brien

*****

"As you know, Trump is being accused of sexual misconduct by a slew of women. Of course, that is a case of 'he said' and 'she said, she said, she said, she said, she said.'"

-- Jimmy Kimmel

*****

"As of a couple of hours ago, Donald Trump hasn't tweeted about his new grandson. He's waiting to see the birth certificate."

-- Jimmy Kimmel

*****

"Trump is unstoppable. He's like Godzilla with less foreign-policy experience."

-- Stephen Colbert

*****

"Donald Trump showed his birth certificate to reporters. Who cares about his birth certificate? I want to know if that thing on his head has had its vaccinations."

-- Craig Ferguson

*****

"You ruined more models' lives than bulimia. You disappointed more women than Sex and the City 2."

-- Lisa Lampanelli

*****

"Jared Kushner wants the government run like a business.

If it's run like his father's business, expect Trump to be in jail soon."

--Nick Jack Pappas

*****

"Trump taps Jared Kushner to lead team that aims to run government like a company, so expect them to refuse to pay bills and file bankruptcy."

-- Michael Blackman

*****

"Trump's Enemies List: 'Everyone but Ivanka.'"

--Erik Bransteen

*****

"In her defense, Kellyanne Conway was misled by the toaster."

--Jeff Dwoskin

*****

"A protester had to be escorted out of the Donald Trump rally last night for yelling, 'Trump's a racist.'   The protester was removed because the Trump campaign has that phrase copyrighted."

--Seth Meyers

*****

"After he won yesterday's Nevada caucus, Donald Trump said, 'I love the poorly educated.' Trump then said, 'And when I'm president there'll be more of them than ever.'"

-- Conan O'Brien

"Over the weekend, three pages of Donald Trump's 1995 tax return were leaked, revealing that he declared a $916 million loss from his three Atlantic City casinos. That's right. Donald Trump lost money on casinos. You know what they say, 'The house always loses.'"

-- Stephen Colbert

"[Trump] said he's sick and tired of the rest of the world laughing at the United States. Well, President Trump will certainly put an end to that!"

-- David Letterman

AND A HALF DOZEN FROM OTHER POLITICIANS:

"Donald Trump has had several foreign wives. It turns out there really are jobs Americans won't do."

--Mitt Romney

*****

"Donald has attacked every person of color, except John Boehner."

--Joe Biden

*****

"Donald Trump is here tonight. Now, I know that he's taken some flak lately. But no one is happier -- no one is prouder -- to put this birth certificate matter to rest than The Donald. And that's because he can finally get back to focusing on the issues that matter. Like did we fake the moon landing? What really happened in Roswell? And where are Biggie and Tupac?"

--Barack Obama

*****

"But folks, on a serious point, Trump said he likes people who don't get captured. What a terrible thing to say about my friend and a genuine war hero, John McCain. So tonight I call on Donald Trump to be a man of his word -- and release Chris Christie right now."

--Joe Biden

*****

"Donald Trump likes to sue people. He should sue whoever did that to his face."

--Marco Rubio

*****

"Donald looks at the Statue of Liberty and sees a four. Maybe a five if she loses the torch and tablet and changes her hair."

--Hillary Clinton

3

ORIGINAL POETRY BY "DONALD TRUMP"

I heard that Jimmy Carter published a book of his original poetry. Give me a break! I can write better poems than that moron, I can tell you that. I am so, so, poetic. Believe me. I can write the best poems. I can write poems that everyone will like, even the poorly educated. Because I love the poorly educated.

Wherever I go they love Trump.
I can con all the rubes on the stump.
They elected me Chief.
And now, to be brief,
On the country I'm taking a dump.

Day one, to restore law and order,
I shall build a great wall on the border.
I will make it with brick
That's as hard as my dick,
And I'll mix all my jizz in the mortar.

The refugees coming from Syria
Are giving me fits of hysteria.
I know, yes I know,
They need someplace to go.
But what the hell's wrong with Algeria?

That psycho buffoon Kim Jong Un,
Will have long-range missiles quite soon.
And you know, if they fly,
Californians will die.
For me, that will be a huge boon.

I am winning, and winning again.
That's why I'm the proudest of men.
Now I am the President.
Of the White House I'm resident.
And my daughter Ivanka's a ten!

With Putin I'm having disputes.
I say he and Assad are both brutes.
Vlad expresses his qualms,
Then I send in some bombs,
Just to show we are not in cahoots.

My tax return? I won't reveal it.
I'll stonewall and lie to conceal it.
If you're so keen to know
Where I get all my dough,
Here's a hint: for the most part, I steal it.

When Obamacare's gone 'twill relieve me.
We will have a great plan then – believe me!
Tax cuts for the wealthy,
The poor better stay healthy.
If they don't, and they die, it won't grieve me.

ODE TO MY HAIR

I have the most glorious hair.
It is golden and shiny and fair.
It flows like the Seine!
If you don't like my mane
You can kiss my big fat *derriere*.

ODE TO MY WIFE

My wife is a belle from Slovenia.
Folks thought she might have schizophrenia.
It was crazy as hell
When she copied Michelle.
Her speech writer's now in Armenia.

ODE TO MY CHILDREN

Ivanka's a lollapaloozer.
If she wasn't my daughter, I'd choose her.
And Barron is cute,
Don Jr.'s a beaut,
But Eric's a bit of a loser.

What's that? I left one out? No, I don't think I did.

WHY CAN'T WE USE THEM?

If we have nuclear weapons, why can't we use them?
Somebody hits us within ISIS -- you wouldn't fight back with nukes?
Then why are we making them? Why do we make them? We have
nuclear capability. I'm not going to take any cards off the table. You
want to be unpredictable with nuclear weapons. I think, for me
nuclear is just the power. The devastation is very important to me.
The devastation is very important to me. Why can't we use them?
Why? Why? I'm going
to bomb the shit out of
them. You want to be
unpredictable. For me,
nuclear is the power.
The devastation is
very important to me.
You wouldn't fight back
with nukes? If we have
nuclear weapons why
can't we use them? Why
do we make them? Why
can't we use them?
I'm going to bomb the
shit out of them.
If we have nuclear weapons, why can't
we use them? Why? The devastation is
very important to me.
I'm going to bomb the
I'm going to bomb the
I'm going to bomb the
shit out of them.

[From actual statements made by DJT]

4

ORIGINAL ARTWORK BY "DONALD TRUMP"

I heard that George W. Bush published a book with his original artwork. Give me a break! I can do art better than that moron. I'm very, very good at art. But my art is kind of deep, so I'll give simple explanations, so simple even the poorly educated can understand them. Because I love the poorly educated.

Can you tell what this is?

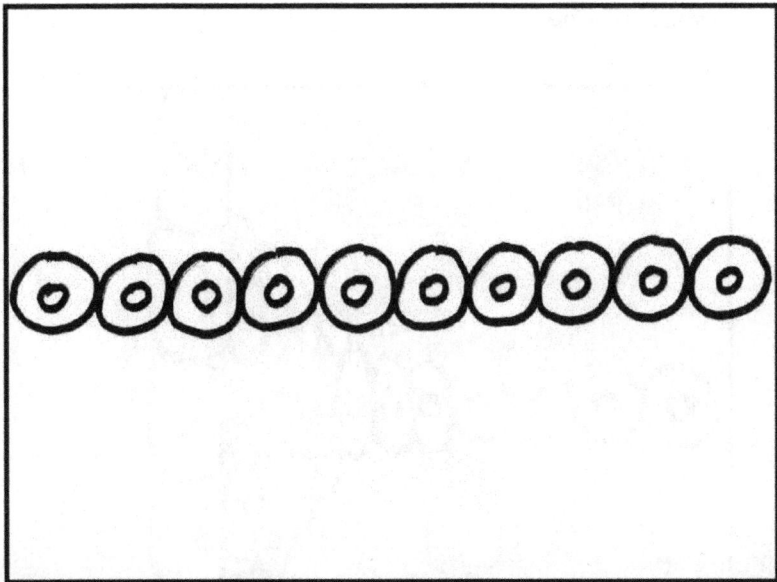

This is a line of Mexicans, headed for the border, as seen from a border patrol helicopter.

How about this?

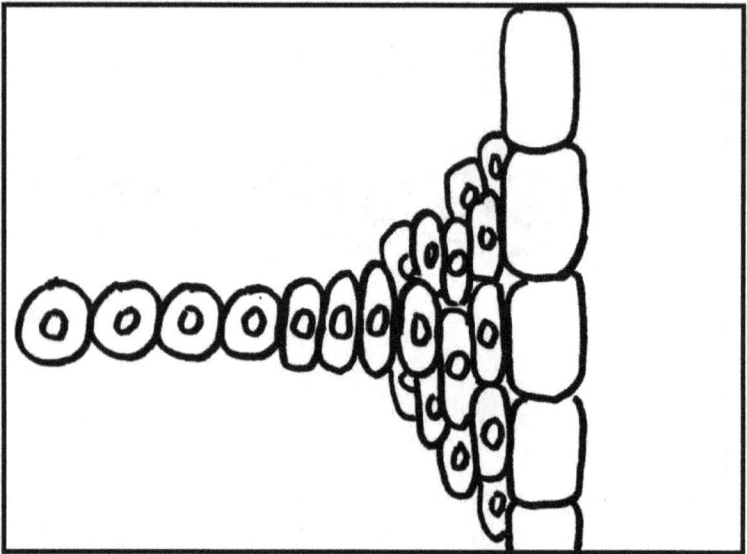

This is the Mexicans, stopped by my big, beautiful wall (as seen from above).

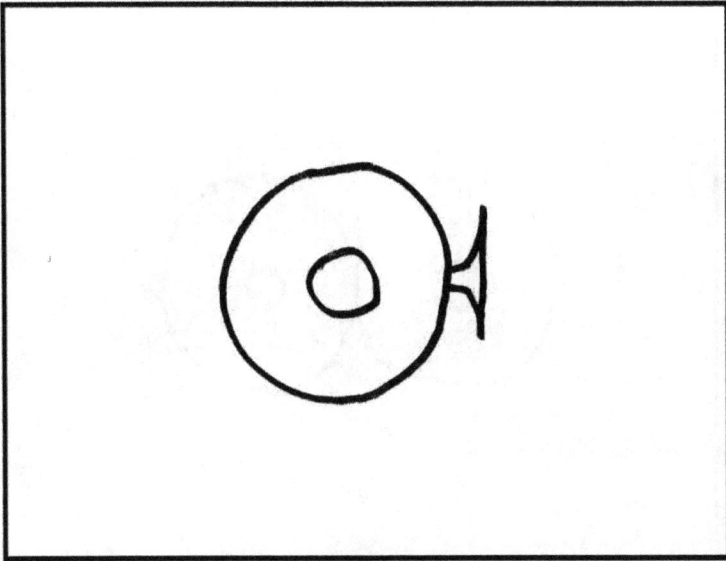

Mariachi trumpet player

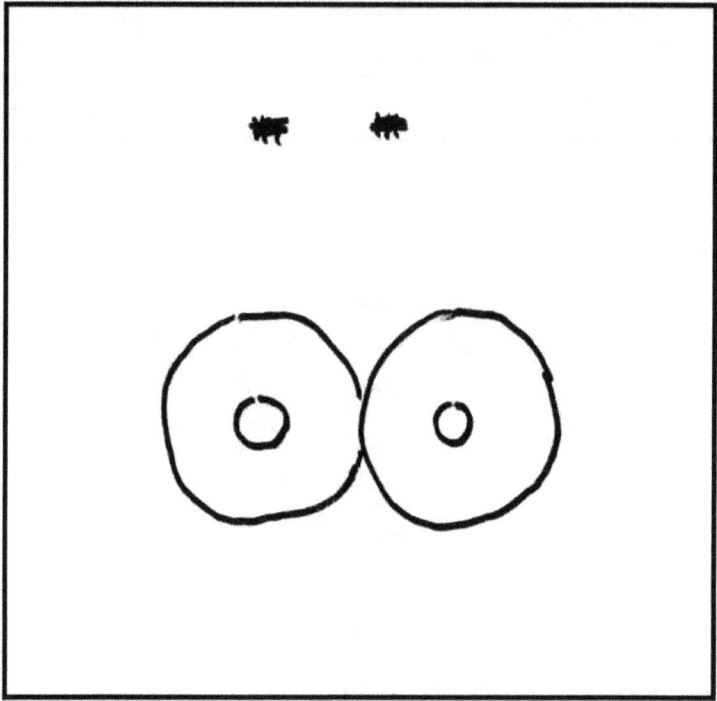

Two Mexicans and two *cucarach*....no, wait. This is my drawing of Melania (as I see her).

Here's another one. It's really, really deep.

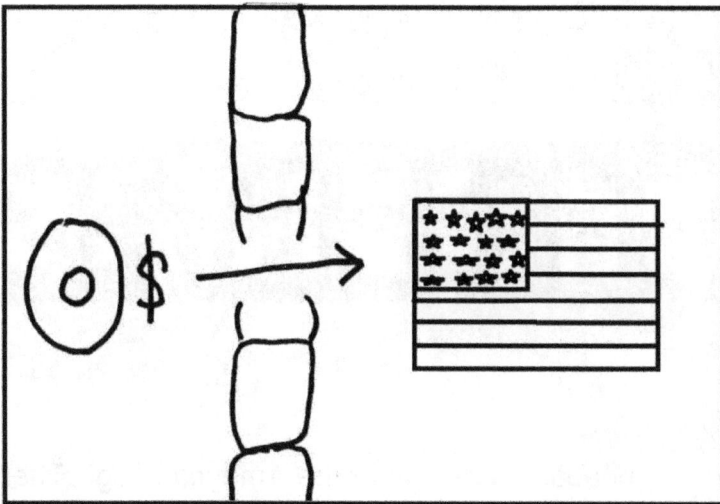

This represents Mexico paying us for the wall.
It uses symbolism, which is very smart, showing I have a
very good brain.

My very beautiful redesign of the American flag. The 30 stars stand for the 30 states that voted for me in the 2016 election. Sorry losers! I don't know what the stripes stand for. Nobody does.

Self portrait.

5

PRESIDENT TRUMP WALKED INTO A BAR, AND
EVEN MORE TRUMP JOKES

PRESIDENT TRUMP WALKED INTO A BAR.

So they lowered it.

*****

Q: What's the difference between a lightbulb and America under the Trump Administration?

A: A lightbulb can be unscrewed.

*****

Trump shows up at Trump Tower late one night, and finds Melania in bed with a Secret Service agent.

Trump screams, "Melania! What are doing?"

Melania turns to the agent, and says, "See? I tuld you he vas an idiot."

*****

Donald and Melania are attending a White House gala, and Melania is wearing her best jewelry. The Vice President's wife, Karen Pence, notices Melania's diamond ring.

"Oh, my," says Mrs. Pence. "That is the most incredible diamond I have ever seen! What an enormous stone!

It's so beautiful."

"Zenk you," says Melania. "Eet eez called ze Trahmp Diamond. Eet eez nearly same size as ze Hope Diamond, and only one carat smaller zen Star Of India. But unfortunately, like Hope Diamond and Star of India, it cahms with a curse."

"Oh?" says Mrs. Pence. "What is the curse?"

Melania sighs, and says, "Doanald."

*****

The top-ranked women's golfer in the United States, Lexi Thompson, played 18 holes at Mar-a-Lago with Donald Trump one day. Afterward, a friend met her in the locker room.

"How was it, playing golf with the President of the United States?" said the friend.

"Disturbing," said Lexi. "I lost."

"That's impossible!" said her friend. "You're the top American in the LPGA. I know Donald Trump is a fairly good amateur golfer, but I would have guessed you would beat him by at least 20 strokes."

"I would've thought so, too," said Lexi. "Especially since he offered to play for money, and I accepted. He said that given the fact that I am a pro golfer, I should at least give him a handicap. He said, 'just give me two gotchas.' I didn't know what a gotcha was, I thought it might be like a gimme, so I agreed.

"On the first tee, he hit a drive of about 150 yards. I thought, this is going to be easy. I got up to hit my drive, addressed the ball, and at the top of my backswing Trump lunged at me, grabbed me by the pussy, and yelled, 'Gotcha!' I shanked the drive."

"Sure," said the friend. "But that was only one stroke, and he only had one gotcha left."

"True," said Lexi. "But can you imagine what it's like trying to swing at a golf ball not knowing when someone's going to grab you by the pussy?"

*****

The Pope dies, and several days later, Donald Trump dies. At the gates of heaven, the Pope is kept waiting, while Trump is sent right in. The Pope doesn't understand, so he asks St. Peter why he, the Pope, is kept waiting, while someone like Trump goes right in.

"Well," says St. Peter, "you'll definitely be getting in at some point, but we have our priorities. You see, when you were chosen as Pope, we didn't see any really big changes. But when Trump was elected President, we couldn't believe how many people started praying!"

*****

President Trump was giving a speech in the ballroom of an exclusive New York club. As Trump approached the podium, one member of the club who didn't much care for Trump snuck out the back door of the ballroom, and went to the bar to get a drink. He stayed in the bar drinking for two hours, then went back to the ballroom.

When he got back inside the ballroom, he was surprised to see that Trump was still speaking. He whispered to another member, "Has he been talking this whole time?"

"Yep," said the other member.

"What's his topic?"

"I don't know. He's still introducing himself."

*****

Reince Priebus entered the Oval Office, where Trump was tweeting about how disgusting Rosie O'Donnell is.

"Excuse me, Mr. President," said Priebus.

"What is it, Reince?" said Trump. "I'm very busy right now."

"It's about the Abortion Bill, sir."

"Oh, for cryin' out loud," said Trump. "Just pay it."

*****

The President is in his office at Trump Tower, talking on the phone to Paul Ryan about the Republican health care bill. Trump's son, Barron, enters the room quietly and sits down.

Trump tells Ryan that he absolutely must get the House to pass the bill, right away. Ryan says that it's impossible, they simply do not have the votes, and it would be best to pull the bill. Trump loses his temper.

"Douchebag!" he yells, and slams the phone down.

Just then, Trump notices Barron.

"I didn't see you come in son," says Trump. "Now, you just heard your daddy say a very nasty word. I was angry, but that's no excuse. It's a very rude word that people shouldn't use. And I don't want to ever hear you using that word."

Barron looks at his father and says, "Too late, douchebag."

*****

Reince Priebus enters the Oval Office, where he finds the President at his desk, finishing a jigsaw puzzle.

"I am so good at this," says Trump. "Look, I'm almost done, and it only took me two weeks!"

"Is that good?" says Priebus.

"Well, just look at the box, Reince," says Trump. "It says 4 to 5 years!"

Donald Trump is worried about how his administration is failing, so one night he goes for a walk and tries to get inspiration. He stops at the Washington monument.

"What should I do George?" he asks.

To his great surprise, he hears a deep voice coming from the monument.

"Be honest," says the voice. "Keep your promises. You promised health care for all. Get it done!"

Wow, thinks Trump. I'm so amazing, I actually got advice from George Washington! He continues on to the Jefferson Memorial.

"Do you have any advice for me, Thomas?"

He hears another resounding voice, saying, "America should never be all about wealthy financiers. Stop favoring Wall Street!"

This is unbelievable, thinks Trump. The greatest presidents are paying attention to me. He heads to the Lincoln Memorial.

"So, Abe," he says. "Got any advice for me?"

"Yes," says an eerie voice. "You've been working too hard. Take tomorrow evening off and go to the theater."

*****

When Trump was running the Miss Universe Pageant, he took one of the contestants back to his hotel room. When he took off his suit and shirt, the young woman said, "My goodness. You certainly are a very large man, aren't you?"

Trump winked at her and said, "What you're seeing is 250 pounds of pure dynamite, baby."

Then Trump dropped his pants and took off his underwear. The girl went running out of the room.

Later, Trump ran into her at the pageant. He took her aside.

"Why did you suddenly run away?" he asked.

"I felt in danger," she said. "All that dynamite, and such a short fuse!"

*****

Trump is in a seaplane, flying from Naples to Mar-a-Lago. As he is flying over the Everglades, he looks down and sees two white guys in a boat, in the middle of a lake. They have a rope tow out the back of the boat, and at the end of the rope tow a black guy with water skis is in the water, waiting.

"Fly a little closer," says Trump to the pilot. Trump looks at the boat with a pair of binoculars, and is pleased to see a "Trump for President" sticker on the boat. He instructs the pilot to land the seaplane.

Trump opens the door of the seaplane, and says to the guys in the boat, "A lot people have the mistaken idea that my supporters down here are racists. Wrong! Here you are, good Trump voters, white guys, taking your black friend waterskiing. Tremendous! I just wanted to thank you guys for proving how unfair the liberals are when they say my voters are racist. Have fun waterskiing, and thank you!"

As the seaplane flies away, one of the guys in the boat turns to the other and says, "Well, he may be the president, and I voted fer him, but he don't know jackshit about huntin' alligator."

*****

Q: Why does Donald Trump take Valium?

A: For Hispanic attacks.

*****

Donald Trump has plans for the country to produce and burn a lot more coal.

He's going to make America gray again.

*****

Eric Trump and Donald Trump, Jr. were the guests of honor at an elite New York hunting club. The club met in a very formal old room, with dark walnut paneling, leather chairs, brass lamps, Persian rugs, and impressive game mounted on the walls. The Club President, a distinguished older gentleman, introduced the Trump brothers.

"As you know, Eric and Donald, Jr. are very accomplished big-game hunters. I am sure you have seen photographs of these two brave fellows with their trophies. I have asked them here today to speak to us. They have very generously agreed to interrupt their busy schedules to tell us about one of their most exciting hunting adventures. Gentlemen?"

The club members applauded, and Eric stood up to speak.

"I am going to tell you about one time when my brother and I were hunting in deepest Africa. It was nighttime, and our guides were leading us across the savanna, in pitch darkness. All we could see was the guides' flickering torches. All we could hear was the distant trumpeting of the elephants. Occasionally, a snake of some kind slithered across the path in front of us. We came to a clearing, and without warning, the largest, most ferocious lion I have ever seen leapt out in front of us, reared up onto his hind legs, and he went, 'RRRROOOOAAAARRRRR!!!'"

Eric sat down. The Club President stood and said, "Oh, please, don't stop. You have us all on tenterhooks. Please tell us, what happened then?"

Eric looked around the room. "I hate to admit it," he said, "but I shit in my pants."

"Come, come," said the Club President. "You don't mean

to tell us that an experienced hunter such as yourself would react that way to a mere lion."

"Oh, no," said Eric. "Not *then*. Just *now*. When I went, 'RRRROOOOAAAARRRRR!!!'"

*****

Trump, to the reporters at a press conference: "I am here today to announce that the F.B.I. has discovered tangible evidence that absolutely proves, beyond a doubt, that Obama personally had me illegally wire tapped during the election campaign."

Reporter: "Really?"

Trump: "Oh, why bring that up?"

*****

BREAKING NEWS: A fire today destroyed President Trump's personal library. Both books were destroyed. Tragically, he had not finished coloring one of them yet.

*****

Q: What did Donald Trump get on his IQ test?

A: Drool.

Q: Why does Sean Spicer like to hang out in the Oval Office?

A: Because he figures the press can't corner him there.

One sunny morning at Mar-a-Lago, Donald Trump was walking from the hotel to the first tee of the golf course, when he saw a young boy dragging something behind him.

"What have you got there, kid?" said Trump.

"Chicken wire," said the boy. "I'm gonna' go catch me some chickens."

"That's stupid, kid," said Trump. "You can't catch chickens with chicken wire."

After Trump finished his round of golf, and was walking back to the hotel, he saw the boy, carrying a couple of chickens.

The next morning, Trump was headed out for his round of golf, when he saw the same boy, dragging something long and thin behind him.

"What have you got there, today?" said Trump.

"Duck tape," said the boy. "I'm gonna' go get me some ducks."

"Don't be an idiot, kid," said Trump. "You can't catch ducks with duck tape."

As Trump was walking from the 18th green, he saw the boy walking back to the hotel, carrying a couple of ducks.

The next morning, Trump was on the first fairway when he saw the boy, carrying a handful of pussy willow.

"Wait up, kid," said Trump. "I'm coming with you."

*****

Reince Priebus came to the Oval Office.

"Mr. President," said the Chief of Staff, "we've just received a report that three Brazilian soldiers have been killed."

"That's terrible," said Trump. "That's a disaster. A total disaster. That's the worst thing I ever heard. We have to figure out a way to blame it on Obama. Such a tragedy."

As Priebus was leaving the office, Trump said, "By the way, Reince, how many is a brazilion?"

*****

We have finally reached complete consensus about something in the United States. A recent poll shows that 100% of Americans believe that, in the 2016 election, 50% of Americans were out of their minds.

*****

Q: What's Donald Trump's favorite pick-up line?

A: "If you were in Mexico, I would never build the wall."

*****

Q: What's Donald Trump's second favorite pick-up line?

A: "Did anyone ever tell you that you look like my daughter?"

*****

A man is walking along the beach in California one day when he sees something shiny in the sand. He picks it up and brushes the sand off of it. It turns out to be a brass lamp, and, of course, a genie appears.

"You have freed me from a thousand years of imprisonment," says the genie. "For that, I will grant you a wish. Ask for anything, and it shall be yours."

"Okay," says the man, "I'll tell you what. I was just walking along, thinking that I have never been to Hawaii. I get seasick, so I cannot go by boat. I am terrified of flying, so I cannot go by plane. I was afraid I would never be able to go to Hawaii. So, my wish is that you build a highway from California to Hawaii, so I can drive there."

"Dear me," says the genie. "I don't think you realize what you are asking for. It is thousands of miles to Hawaii. The Pacific Ocean is miles deep. There is not enough concrete in the world to build a highway from California to Hawaii. Plus, consider the engineering problems involved, the curvature of the earth, the unstable seabed, tidal waves, cyclones. What you are asking is an impossibility. I know I promised you could ask for anything, but you must be more realistic. Make another wish."

"All right," says the man. "Earlier today I was thinking that I do not understand what happened in the 2016 election. My wish is that you explain to me, in a rational way that I can understand, how Americans could have elected that man to be president of the United States."

The genie thinks for a moment, then says, "So... do you want two lanes or four?"

*****

Kellyanne Conway wanted to go to Best Buy to get a new TV set, but she did not want to be assailed by the media or other pests, so she put on an elaborate disguise.

At the store, a salesperson offered to help her.

"I would like to buy this TV set," said Kellyanne.

The salesperson said, "You're Kellyanne Conway, aren't you?"

"This is such a good disguise," said Kellyanne. "How could you tell it was me?"

"Because that's a microwave."

*****

Donald Trump dies and goes to heaven. St. Peter meets him at the gates.

"It's actually a tremendous relief that I got here, I can tell you that," says Trump.

"It's not an entirely done deal," says St. Peter. "In fact, it's going to be your decision. The way it works is, you get to experience the other place for a day, then come back and take a look at heaven, then decide where you would rather spend eternity."

"I can't imagine there's much of a decision to be made," says Trump. "But I'm flexible. I'm actually very proud of my flexibility."

The next thing he knows, Trump wakes up in hell. He looks around, expecting to see fire and brimstone and terrible suffering. But instead, he finds himself in a luxurious hotel room, larger and more beautifully decorated than the Honeymoon Suite at Mar-a-Lago. It smells like roses. Uniformed waiters wheel in carts loaded with mouthwatering desserts. Beautiful, scantily-clad models come into the room and give him an exquisite massage.

Next, Trump walks outside to see the grounds, where he is joined by throngs of adoring fans, who tell him what a great leader he was, and how wonderful he looks. They lead him to the golf course, which is by far the most fantastic course he has ever seen. He plays a round, during which he can do no wrong. Every drive is straight, every putt drops. After the round, he is met by all of his friends who predeceased him, who throw him a spectacular welcoming party, with famous entertainers, and a fireworks display in his honor. He goes to bed with a huge smile on his face.

The next morning, he wakes up back in heaven. He looks around. It looks like a nice place, peaceful and pleasant, but sort of plain and dull after what he experienced the day before. St. Peter walks up and asks him if he's made a decision.

"No offense, Pete," says Trump, "but since it's my choice, I'm going with the other place."

Trump finds himself getting drowsy, and falls asleep. He wakes up to the smell of sulfur, and the sound of agonized screams. It's unbearably hot. He opens his eyes, and looks around. He is surrounded by flames and hideous-looking gargoyles. Satan walks up to him.

"What gives?" says Trump. "This isn't anything like the place I saw yesterday."

"Yesterday was the campaign," says Satan. "Today, you voted."

*****

The President is walking across the Washington Mall one day when he sees a small boy looking intently into a cardboard box. Trump hears faint mewing coming from the box.

Trump looks down at the boy, and says, "What have you got in the box, kid?"

"Newborn kittens," says the boy. "They're only a day old."

"Aw, that's cute," says Trump. "But tell me this. Are they Republican kittens?"

"Yes, sir," says the boy.

"Good," says Trump. He walks away.

A few days later, Trump is walking across the Mall with Chuck Schumer. Trump sees the boy with the cardboard box, in the same place as before. He thinks of a way he can one-up Schumer. He walks Schumer over to the boy.

"Have you got some kittens in that box?" says Trump.

"Yes, sir," says the boy.

"Tell my friend, Senator Schumer, what kind of kittens they are."

"They're Democrat kittens," says the boy.

"Wait a minute, kid," says Trump. "A few days ago, you said they were Republicans."

"Yes," says the boy. "But since then, their eyes have opened."

*****

There is a term for presidents like Donald Trump.

Hopefully, not two...

*****

Trump, to Pence: "The less immigrants we let in, the better."

Pence: "The fewer."

Trump: "I told you not to call me that in public."

*****

Q: What will Trump do with his nukes when he figures he doesn't need them anymore?

A: Fire them.

*****

Barack Obama wrote a best-selling book called, *Dreams of My Father.*

Donald Trump wants to write a book like that, only he's going to call his, *Dreams of My Daughter.*

*****

Donald Trump has already solved America's immigration crisis.

Since he got elected, nobody wants to sneak into the United States anymore.

*****

John, writing the Book of Revelation: "What sayest thou, my Lord? The end will be signaled by trumpets?"

God: "No, I said Trump/Pence."

John: "Got it. That's 'trumpets.'"

God: "No, I said...never mind. When the time comes, they'll know."

*****

After Ivanka Trump had been dating Jared Kushner for awhile, she invited Jared over to meet her father. At the end of the evening, Jared left, and Ivanka asked her father what he thought of Jared.

"He seems to be a nice young man," said Trump. "But I wonder about his influence on you, because, you know, he's Jewish."

"Jewish?" said Ivanka. "What *schmuck* told you that?"

*****

The lifeguard at the Mar-a-Lago swimming pool asked to speak privately with the President.

"I know you own the place, sir," said the lifeguard. "But with all due respect, I have to ask you to please stop urinating in the pool."

"Why?" said Trump. "Everybody pees in the pool."

The lifeguard said, "Yes, sir, but not from the diving board."

*****

Melania and two other women members of Mar-a-Lago go into the women's locker room, and are shocked to see a man in one of the shower stalls. Because of the door on the stall, and a bench in front of it, they can only see him from his waist to his knees.

One of the women says, "Well! I can certainly tell you that he isn't *my* husband!"

The second woman says, "Well, he isn't *my* husband, either!"

Melania says, "Sheet! He nut even member of thees club!"

*****

"Kiss me."

"No, I can't."

"Come on."

"I shouldn't."

"Why not?"

"It just doesn't seem right."

"Why?"

"Because I'm your father, Ivanka. We probably shouldn't even be screwing."

*****

The White House physician says to President Trump, "I just examined Melania, and I must tell you that your wife has acute angina."

Trump says, "You're telling me!"

*****

A grade school teacher notices that one of her students,

a little boy named Henry, appears to be glum.

"Is something wrong, Henry?" says the teacher.

Henry says, "I didn't get no breakfast."

"That's a shame," says the teacher. "But we need to go on with our lessons. Today we're going to be talking about current events. Now, I'm sure you've heard that President Trump is talking about building a wall on the Mexican border. Can you tell me where the Mexican border is?"

Henry says, "He's in my mom's room. That's why I didn't get no breakfast."

*****

President Trump asks his Secretary of Defense, General Mattis, what option he recommends for responding to Syria's chemical weapons attack on its citizens.

Mattis says, "Our response should be proportional. We could hit the airfield from which the chemical weapons attack was launched with 50 to 100 Tomahawks."

"Okay," says Trump. "But wouldn't it be better to use missiles?"

*****

Q: What's the difference between Steve Bannon and a sperm?

A: A sperm has a one in 200 million chance of someday being a human being.

*****

Clint Eastwood is making a movie about Donald Trump. It's called "Billion Dollar Cry Baby."

*****

Donald Trump is having lunch with Marco Rubio at Mar-a-Lago. Things have been awkward between the two leaders ever since the 2016 campaign.

"I hope," says Rubio, "there's no hard feelings, particularly about the jokes I made about the size of your, you-know-what."

"You were way out of line with that," says Trump. "In fact, I'm going to make you a bet. I'll bet you $1000 that mine is longer soft than yours is hard."

"That's a ridiculous bet," says Rubio. "It's biologically impossible for yours to be longer soft than mine is hard."

"Are you afraid to take the bet, little Marco?" says Trump.

"Okay," says Rubio. "You're on. How long is yours soft?"

Trump sighs, and says, "Five years."

*****

Trump is walking along the sidewalk in New York City one day, accompanied by Secret Service agents. As he passes by a construction site behind a high plywood wall, he hears the construction workers on the other side of the wall chanting, "Ten! Ten! Ten!"

"I know New York City construction workers," says Trump. "They know a good looking broad when they see one. For them to be chanting like that, there must be a real babe walking by over there. I've gotta' get a look at this."

He notices a knothole in the plywood wall, and puts his eye up to it. A sharp stick pokes him in the eye.

The workers start chanting, "Eleven! Eleven! Eleven!"

*****

Donald Trump was riding in his chauffeur-driven limousine through Iowa one day when a pig ran out in the road and was struck by the limo.

"Oh, dear," said the chauffeur. "I believe I have struck a pig with the limousine, sir."

"That's terrible," said Trump. "A terrible mess. This happened because of Obama's failure to improve our infrastructure. You better get out and check on the pig."

The chauffeur got out, walked over to where the pig was lying, then came back to the limo.

"I'm afraid I have killed the poor animal, sir," said the chauffeur.

"That's a disaster," said Trump. "Another terrible mess caused by Obama. I inherited a mess, and bad infrastructure that caused that poor pig to be killed. You better go up to the farmhouse and tell the owners that you killed their pig."

The chauffeur walked up the long driveway, and knocked on the door of the farmhouse. Several minutes later, he walked back down the driveway toward the limousine, carrying two bottles of champagne, his face covered with lipstick smudges.

"What happened?" said Trump.

The chauffeur said, "I told them that I'm President Trump's driver, and I just killed the pig."

*****

During the presidential campaign, Donald and Melania attended the Iowa State Fair. The state fair had one of those quaint, old-fashioned scales that give you your weight and fortune for a penny.

"Theese eez so cute," said Melania. "Pliz get on scale, Doanald. Let's see vaht eet says."

Donald got on the scale, and one of his aides put a penny in the machine. A moment later, the machine spit out a small card. Melania pulled out the card and looked at it.

"Eet says you are netchurel born leader, weeth fine character, and attracteeve to veemen."

She flipped the card over. "Hmm. Eet has your vate wrong, also."

*****

At a campaign town hall meeting, Trump was talking to a prospective voter.

"After I'm elected," Trump said, "you will be eating caviar and drinking champagne every day."

"I don't like caviar and champagne," said the voter.

"After I'm elected," said Trump, "you *will* like it."

*****

At a press conference, Trump is taking questions from the reporters.

An aggressive reporter from CNN asks, "What do you have to say to people who are concerned that all of your decisions are controlled by powerful special interests?"

"I will thank you," says Trump, "to leave my daughter and son-in-law out of this."

*****

Two elderly Jewish men meet for breakfast. As they sit down at the table, one of them says, "Oy, vey!"

The other one says, "Look, if you're going to talk about Trump, I'm out of here."

*****

An article appears in *Rolling Stone* saying that Donald Trump appears to know little or nothing about music, and from what is known about Trump's interest in music, it seems that he has very poor taste. Trump hears about the article and is extremely upset.

"How can they say that?" says Trump. "I probably know more about music than any president ever. And I have the best taste. The best. This is the dishonest, lying media at its worst. They're terrible people. Total scum. I'll show them. I'll make them eat those words."

So Trump uses some of his great wealth to rent Carnegie Hall, and to hire a famous symphony orchestra to perform a Beethoven symphony, which Trump himself intends to conduct. He figures these are great musicians, how hard can it be to stand in front of them and wave a baton in time to the music? I will be the first president ever to conduct a symphony orchestra, playing a great symphony at Carnegie Hall. Then we'll see what they have to say about my musical knowledge and taste.

As the concert begins, the musicians in the orchestra quickly realize that Trump has no idea how to conduct, so each of them just tries to play his or her part as best they can. As the first movement of the symphony goes on, however, the musicians get farther and farther out of sync with each other. The dissonance gets worse and worse, until the musicians can hardly stand it.

Finally, one of the percussionists decides he must put an end to this travesty. He picks up the cymbals, and, in a particularly quiet moment in the piece, slams the cymbals together in an earsplitting, resounding crash that silences the orchestra, and echoes through the concert hall.

Trump puts down his baton, looks around the orchestra, and says, "Okay. Which one of you assholes did that?"

*****

Donald Trump and Marco Rubio are hanging out at the bar at Mar-a-Lago. "You know, little Marco," Trump says, "you gave me a lot of heat during the primaries about my ridiculously tiny, itty-bitty hands. Which I think was very unfair, by the way. Tremendously unfair. But I bet you've been wondering how I got these ridiculously tiny, itty-bitty hands."

"Yes," says Rubio, "I actually was wondering about that."

"Well," says Trump, "as a young man, I was walking along the beach when I saw a lamp buried in the sand. I rubbed it, and a genie came out, who offered to grant me three wishes."

"Wow!" says Rubio. "What did you wish for?"

Trump says, "First, I wished to be wealthy. And I am, you know, incredibly wealthy. I've had tremendous success.

And I've never even had to pay any income t..." Trump stops and clears his throat.

"Anyway," he continues, "second, I wished to be powerful. Which I am, you know. I'm president, like you and the other losers wanted to be."

Trump pauses to take a sip of his virgin piña colada. "Third," he says, "and I think this is where I made my mistake -- I wished for ridiculously tiny, itty-bitty hands."

*****

BREAKING NEWS: The F.B.I has just foiled a terrorist plot to assassinate the President. The terrorists were planning to use a surface-to-hair missile.

*****

Trump: "Bill Maher has been saying that I look like an orangutan. Wrong! Wrong! Orangutans look like *me*."

*****

Q: What does G.O.P. stand for?

A: Grabs Our Pussies.

*****

Q: What's the difference between a porcupine and the Oval Office?

A: A porcupine has the prick on the outside.

*****

The restaurant at Mar-a-Lago is featuring a new dessert. It's called the Trump Torte. It is extremely rich, but it has no taste.

*****

Eric Trump calls up his father one day and says he has decided he wants to be an F.B.I agent.

"I saw a movie about an F.B.I agent. It looks really cool. Can you set that up for me?"

"Sure," says the Donald. "I'm the President. They have to do what I say."

Trump calls up the F.B.I Director, James Comey, and tells him that Eric wants to be an agent.

"Can you make that happen, Jim?"

"I suppose so," says Comey. "But you know, he will have to take an I.Q. test."

"Hmmm," says Trump. "That could be complicated. Who knew it was so complicated? Can't you just give him a test that you're sure he'll pass?"

"Well, I don't know..."

"Or, I could send out a tweet about how Rudy wired up your announcement on Hillary's emails."

"I'll administer the test myself," says Comey.

Eric comes to Comey's office to take the test.

"Question one," says the Director, "how much is two plus two?"

"Four," says Eric.

"Correct!" says Comey. "And what is the square root of four?"

"Um, er..."

"Rhymes with shoe."

"Um...two?" says Eric.

"Right again!" says Comey. "Just one more question. Who killed John F. Kennedy?"

"I dunno."

"Well, you can go home and think about it. Do some research, if you need to. Come back tomorrow."

When Eric gets home, he gets a call from his father.

"Well, son," says Trump, "did you get the job?"

"Oh, yeah," says Eric, "and not only that. They've already got me working on a big murder case!"

*****

Trump, working from the Winter White House at Mar-a-Lago, calls up his Secretary of Housing, Ben Carson.

"Hello, this is Dr. Carson, brain surgeon."

"Ben, it's me. The President."

Silence on the line.

"Of the United States."

"Oh, right," says Carson. "That still blows my mind. What can I do you for?"

"I need you down here at Mar-a-Lago for a meeting tomorrow morning at 9:00 a.m., sharp."

"Sure, Mr. Prez," says Carson. "Should I bring my electrodes, to stimulate your brain?"

"No, Ben. I have a very good brain. We're going to talk about housing."

"Housing?"

"You're my Secretary of Housing."

"I knew that."

"I'll arrange a room for you here at the resort. And don't forget your luggage."

The next morning at nine, Trump is waiting in the dining room at Mar-a-Lago, where he holds his most important meetings. There's no sign of Carson. Trump knows what room he's in, and calls it.

"Dr. Carson, brain surgeon, speaking."

"Ben, it's me. The President. It's after nine. Why the hell aren't you here?"

"I can't get out of my room."

"Why not?"

"Well, there's only three doors in the room. One is the closet. Another is the bathroom. And the third one has a sign hanging on the doorknob that says, 'Do Not Disturb.'"

6

WHAT DONALD TRUMP THINKS

Donald Trump thinks an Israeli settlement is two cents on the dollar.

*****

Trump thinks the Helsinki Accords are Hondas made in Finland.

*****

Trump thinks the Gaza Strip is a Burlesque act performed by Lady Gaza.

*****

Trump thinks the "Mother of all Bombs" is *Ishtar.*

*****

Donald Trump thinks Taco Bell is the Mexican phone company.

*****

Trump thinks Al Green is a group of environmentalist jihadis.

*****

Donald Trump thinks Irving Berlin is the Jewish part of Germany.

*****

Trump thinks Conway Twitty is an accurate description of Kellyanne.

*****

Donald Trump thinks he is a "tree-hugger" because he used to have sex with Maples.

*****

Donald Trump thinks the Gross National Product is canned vegetables.

*****

Trump thinks a domestic policy is something you buy to ensure that you will have maid service.

*****

Trump thinks *supply curve* is what a good brassiere does.

*****

Trump thinks the Monroe Doctrine is the medical care they gave Marilyn.

*****

Trump thinks NASA is where poor people go to vacation in the Bahamas.

*****

Trump thinks the space program is Star Trek.

*****

Trump thinks a press secretary is a stenographer who also does ironing.

*****

Trump thinks Sunni is Woody Allen's wife/daughter (and he envies him for having one).

*****

Trump thinks Shiite is what Arabs say when they step in camel dung.

.

*****

Trump doesn't know what Kurds are, but he thinks they might have had something to do with the disappearance of Miss Muffet.

*****

Trump thinks Marine Le Pen is a Bic that writes underwater.

*****

Trump thinks Theresa May is a good reason to flirt with Theresa.

*****

Trump thinks Bishopsgate is a Catholic pedophilia scandal.

*****

Trump thinks a "motion to table" is how you get the waiter to bring the check.

*****

Trump thinks *pro tempore* is expertly made Japanese food.

*****

Donald Trump confuses Mexicans with Arabs, because he thinks if you've seen Juan, you've seen Jamal.

*****

Trump thinks the "public option" is to go screw themselves.

*****

Trump thinks *Roe vs. Wade* were the two options Washington had for crossing the Delaware.

*****

Trump thinks he's as smart as Sherlock Holmes, because his tax return has so many amazing deductions.

7

THE LAST DAY OF THE TRUMP ADMINISTRATION

A Short Story

Author's Note: The Trump Administration personnel who are fictionalized in this short story were all working for Trump at the time of this writing. By the time you read this, it is safe to assume that one or more (or, most likely, all) of them will have been fired.

The hazy sunrise burnished the calm Potomac with a golden sheen like that of Donald Trump's now universally admired hair. As the President's staff readied themselves and their offices for the final full day of the Administration's second term, their deep feelings of satisfaction in a job well done, and their robust pride in simply being Americans at such a high-water mark in the country's history was mixed with a tinge of sadness. A wonderful era, and their part in it, was drawing to a close. Their mood at this *denoument,* like that of the entire country, was bittersweet.

All good things must end. Too bad about that 22nd Amendment.

Not that the entire eight years had been smooth, sweet and successful. The early going had been rough, with conflicts, scandals, and suspicions pouring down and piling up around the White House like hailstones. There were even a few tense moments when the President's top advisers feared that the administration would be consumed in a fiery blaze of prosecutions, impeachment, and electoral disaster.

Sean Spicer smiled as he thought back on those tumultuous early months, his recollection triggered by a framed photograph which rested atop the boxful of mementos he had packed to take with him. The photo was of Melissa McCarthy, and it was signed: "To Sean, with warm regards. Thanks for being such a good sport."

"Remember this?" said Sean, holding the photo out to show Kellyanne Conway.

"Oh, for sure," said Kellyanne, with a chuckle. "Wasn't

her impression of you on *Saturday Night Live* hilarious?"

"It really was," said Sean. "Kate McKinnon got you pretty good, too."

"We so had it coming," said Kellyanne. "You with your defensiveness and over-the-top belligerence at those press conferences, and me with my evasiveness and fabrications. Remember 'alternative facts'?"

Sean and Kellyanne laughed heartily and long. It took Sean a moment to catch his breath.

"It was such a relief when the President finally said I should stop treating the press like enemy number one," said Sean. "To just give them the information they needed to do their jobs, and give it in a straight, open and professional way. That sure made my life a whole lot better. I got along with everybody after that, even Melissa McCarthy. I even stopped swallowing 35 pieces of gum a day."

"Tell me about it," said Kellyanne. "Can you imagine how much better I felt when he said I should stop lying every time I did an interview? That I could actually give honest answers that didn't sound idiotic? It meant I didn't have to feel ashamed in front of my family and friends anymore. I could look in a mirror without wanting to throw up."

"The whole country felt a lot better after The Great Makeover," said Sean.

"Everybody except the Before Cabinet," said Kellyanne.

Kellyanne and Sean laughed again, a little nervously.

The Great Makeover was the term the news media

coined to describe the stunning shift in the President's approach to governing that took place late in his first term. The Before Cabinet was what they called the group of billionaires, Wall Street insiders, cronies, flimflammers, and over-the-hill retirees that made up the President's original cabinet. Most of them had been appointed either as a reward for campaign donations or for the risks they took collaborating with a foreign adversary to rig the election, or because they were openly hostile to the goals of the very departments they were appointed to run, and so could be counted on to undermine the work of those departments. Appointing agency heads who would cripple their own agencies was part of the first phase of Steve Bannon's plan to destroy the state.

It didn't take long for the Before Cabinet to louse up the work of the federal government to such a degree that even the President's most ardent supporters could no longer deny that the results were calamitous. The environment, the schools, labor relations, foreign relations, healthcare, consumer protection, food safety, product safety, airline safety -- virtually everything the federal government touched headed downhill fast. Some of the parts of the country that had voted overwhelmingly for the President saw spikes in unemployment, poverty, pollution, environmentally caused illnesses, depression, malnutrition, and even suicide.

The Congress didn't help, either passing legislation that cut back needed programs or, more often, failing to pass legislation to replace programs that the administration had deliberately destroyed.

It was not a pretty picture.

It got so bad that the President drew a challenger for his party's nomination. It did not look good when, in his first debate, his opponent hammered the President with a litany of his failures, blunders, lies and outright delusions, and all the President could say in response, over and over, was, "I know you are but what am I?"

When the President's approval rating hit single digits, even he knew something, no, *everything*, had to change, *bigly*. It was then that Steve Bannon showed the President's inner circle Phase 2 of his plan, which included orchestrating false terror attacks to justify a new Mideast war, severe restrictions on civil liberties, detention camps for "enemies of the administration," and seizure of media assets.

Phase 3? Martial law.

"I wonder if we'll ever find out which one of the Before Cabinet leaked the Bannon Plan to the Washington *Post*," said Kellyanne. "My money's on Mad Dog Mattis."

"Not that it made any difference," said Sean. "The President loved that plan. He had so much dirt on the Republican congressional leaders none of them would have lifted a finger to stop it, and Fox News would've sold it like it was the Second Coming, because they would've been the only broadcast news network left standing."

"I know," said Kellyanne. "Don't forget, I was scheduled to go on Fox and say that the orchestrated terror attack in Bowling Green proved that we were right about that all along, and that it showed that the President was clairvoyant and omniscient, just like he said, and I had to say it all with a straight face."

"Let's face it," said Sean. "What turned it all around and saved us wasn't the leak of the Bannon Plan."

"No," said Kellyanne with a giggle. "It was the leak of Bannon."

At the nadir of the administration, the President's inner circle met at Trump Tower to discuss implementation of Phases 2 and 3 of the Bannon Plan. Coffee and juice were served. Bannon, who had a prostate the size of a grapefruit, had a sudden, extremely urgent need to use the men's room. He bolted from the room, accompanied by Stephen Miller, as the two were locked in an intense discussion of the degree to which ethnicity and religion would be considered in identifying "clients" to be "relocated" to the "involuntary lifestyle communities." Jared Kushner had come up with the terminology.

Bannon and Miller were so absorbed in the debate that neither one noticed that the elevator doors opened on an empty shaft. When their bodies were found five days later, everyone in the White House and Congress realized that Bannon could no longer threaten anyone with the prodigious blackmail he had collected while chief executive of the Government Accountability Institute, the organization he founded to conduct investigations of government officials.

Then, the Great Makeover began. The President guest-hosted a special edition of The Apprentice in which he had every member of the Before Cabinet come to his office so he could tell them, "you're fired." It had the highest ratings in television history. The Before Cabinet was replaced by highly capable, ethical, experienced top experts in the work of their respective departments. Ph.D.'s instead of campaign donors and washed-up politicians. The Bannon Plan was abandoned, along with the slash-and-burn budget and scorched-earth domestic policies from Phase 1.

With the fabric of the nation coming apart at the seams and defeat in the next election a certainty, the President completely changed course, directing the After Cabinet to work with him and congressional leaders of both parties to craft policies reforming entitlements, financial regulation, environmental protection, immigration policy and healthcare. Purged of corrupt cronies and nitwit politicians, the cabinet experts showed the President that, if he based his policies on verifiable data and established principles of good government, solutions to many difficult challenges could be crafted that enjoyed 60% or more public support. But he had to have faith in truth and knowledge. He had to abandon delusion, distraction and division as his primary political tactics, and try to see fair and honest economics, a cleaner environment, and friendly relations with neighboring countries as *good* things.

The President was so desperate and so out of options, he decided what the hell, why not give it a try? What have I got to lose?

No more denying established science, the experts said. No more stirring up false fears and denying real ones. No more cutting poor and elderly food programs to pay for multi-billion dollar handouts to foreign mobsters and Wall Street swindlers.

Okay, okay, okay, said the President.

No more tweeting fabrications to distract people from the real issues, they said.

Aw, come on, said the President. Can't you just give me that one? Well... *alright*.

What followed was an unprecedented era of enlightened policy, honesty in government, and bipartisan cooperation. As it turned out, once he stopped manipulating the ignorant with lies, fears and false promises, and once the swamp was actually drained, the President revealed himself to be a skillful dealmaker, and a charismatic leader. He started putting his media savvy and boundless energy to use for the benefit of 99.9% of Americans, instead of 0.1%.

The economy and the functioning of the government recovered quickly enough for the President to eke out a narrow victory in the next election, and earn a second term. This time, he did it without any help from Russia. Oil prices had tanked, putting the Russian economy into a tailspin and demonstrators into the streets of Moscow. Putin, of course, blamed his country's collapsing economy on the American president, which started a feud between the two leaders. Putin escalated the conflict by releasing the *kompromat* he had on the President, but by that time the President had done so many things to embarrass himself that the American public shrugged off videotapes of golden showers and such.

Then, completely freed from the morass of deception that had characterized the early months of his first term, and out from under the control of Bannon and Putin, the President launched a vigorous, all-out campaign to fulfill all of the promises he had made to working Americans, and to release Washington from the scourge of corruption and the stranglehold of lobbyists.

His administration went from success to success, making great strides in social programs, healthcare, infrastructure, diplomacy, scientific research, and international trade. The quality and efficiency of everything from the judiciary to the military improved dramatically, as did the President's poll numbers. By the end of his second term, his approval rating, middle-class prosperity, consumer confidence, the stock market, and American life expectancy were all at all-time highs.

"He really did make America great again, after all, didn't he?" said Kellyanne.

"Well, *greater*," said Sean. "It was already pretty great."

"We did good, then."

"We did a whole lot of good, for a whole lot of people."

"Then why do I feel so sad? And why do you look so sad?" said Kellyanne. "Is it because we're going to miss this place and these jobs?"

"No," said Sean. "Eight years is more than enough."

"Is it because we were talking about what happened to the Steves? It took so long to find them, they must have been down there suffering for days."

"Nah, that's not it."

"Is it because all of the successes of this administration never happened, and this is just a stupid Shaggy Dog story in a cheap joke book?"

"That's it."

8

THE TRUMP WIT

Among Donald Trump's many notable attributes – flamboyance, brashness, a unique hairstyle – the President is also known to possess an urbane, sophisticated wit. His clever comebacks and rapier-like repartee are destined to become as admired as his statesmanship. A few examples are presented here for your amusement, and to preserve them for posterity.

One story that is told to illustrate Trump's suave wit is the one about the time he and Hillary Clinton had just finished a particularly impolite and hostile debate, during which each had insulted the other, and Trump had said that if he were president, Clinton would be in jail.

Within earshot of the debate attendees, Hillary said indignantly, "Mr. Trump, if I were your wife, I would poison your coffee!"

Not to be outdone, with a twinkle in his eye, Trump replied, "Shove it up your ass, ya' stupid cow."

*****

Another example of the famously sophisticated Trump wit occurred shortly after his inauguration. One of the new president's first visitors was the British ambassador.

Upon observing the President's imposing physical stature, the ambassador asked, "I say, Mr. President, how long do you think a man's legs should be?"

Trump thought for a moment, cocked an eyebrow quizzically, and quipped:

"Fuck should I know?"

Then the President reflected for another moment, cocked the other eyebrow, and added:

"Faggot."

A young female White House intern was invited to a formal State Department banquet. She was delighted, but also a little intimidated, to see that the official seating chart showed that she would be seated right next to the President at dinner.

She told a friend about the seating chart, and her nervousness about making conversation with the President. Her friend bet her that she could not get the President to say more than two words to her during the entire dinner.

At the banquet, the intern was indeed having trouble engaging the President in conversation. Dessert was being served, and he had yet to speak a word to her. She decided to try the direct approach.

"Mr. President," she said, "I have a bet with a friend of mine that I can get you to say more than two words to me at dinner."

The President dabbed at his mouth with his napkin, turned to the young lady, winked at her, and said, "Nice tits."

*****

Another example of Trump's urbane wit and gift for clever repartee is the time he attended a Washington gala with members of Congress and business leaders. Trump rarely consumed alcoholic beverages, but on this occasion he had clearly overindulged. He stumbled into Nancy Pelosi, spilling a glass of champagne on her dress.

"Mr. Trump," said Pelosi, "you are drunk. You are very drunk. You are very, very drunk."

Trump drew himself up to his full height, raised his champagne glass with a debonair flourish, and, with a twinkle in his eye, said, "Yeah, and you're ugly. So fuck off."

*****

At the height of the media frenzy over the Trump campaign's contact with Russian spies, Trump decided he needed a big story to distract attention. Having heard reports of a possible war on the border between Israel and Jordan, he dispatched a White House photographer to get pictures of the conflict.

A few days later, the photographer wired Trump, "There is no war here. I could send you pictures of the scenery, but I can't send you the pictures you want because there is no war."

Ever the master of how the media works, Trump wired back:

"You're fired."

*****

In early 2016, Donald Trump and Marco Rubio were in a tightening race for the Republican nomination. A turning point came in a debate, when Trump questioned whether Rubio, who was then 44 years old, was mature enough to be president. Rubio fired back.

"I am 44 years old, Mr. Trump," said Rubio. "When John F. Kennedy became president, he was only 43."

Trump raised his chin in a dignified manner, and said, slowly and deliberately, "Senator, I knew John Kennedy. John Kennedy was a friend of mine. And believe me, Senator, you are as big an asshole as he was."

BACKWARD

By "Donald Trump"

See? I told you I would write a Backward. Who keeps promises better than me? Nobody, I can tell you that.

People are saying there's a lot of funny jokes in this book. Give me a break. I can make up better jokes, believe me. Really, really great jokes. The best.

Here I go: what's black and white and red all over? Barack Obama, covered in blood. Get it? He's half black, and half white, and it's funny because that would be so funny if Obama was all bloodied for some reason.

Or, better yet, what's *blonde* and white and red all over? Megyn Kelly, bleeding out of her whatever. *Ba-dump-bump.*

Here's another one: why do firemen wear red suspenders? To keep their pants up, so they don't accidentally fuck that disgusting fat pig Rosie O'Donnell. Now *that's* funny, believe me. Jared will love that one. He laughs at everything I say.

How many Mexicans does it take to screw in a lightbulb? Only Juan. I am laughing so hard now. Why did the chicken cross the border? To take a job from an American chicken, and rape hens. Zing! I'm on a roll now, folks.

Why don't they need to build bathrooms in Syria? Because I am going to bomb the shit out of 'em.

Bannon went to the doctor, and it turns out he needs surgery, because he has reince on his priebus. Ha! I don't know what makes Reince such a loser, but it really, really works. *Chortle-chortle.* I kid Reince a lot, but it's all in good fun, and it's okay because he's such a creepy little weirdo. And no matter what they tell you, it's also totally okay to make fun of the handicapped, because I'm not handicapped.

I totally nailed this Backward, didn't I? Totally nailed it.

Enough joking around. I gotta' get back to winning. And whining. And whining and winning. Now, they're telling me Russian tanks are rolling into Ukraine. I better call Vlad and see if they need any help with that.

Also by Marc Brel:

Despots Say the Darndest Things

Stop! You're Killing Me! The Best Practical Jokes of the Spanish Inquisition

The Sound and the Führer: How Hitler Amused the Reichstag with Flatulence Noises

The Lighter Side of the Gulag Archipelago

Who's There?   101 Knock-knocks Used by the Gestapo

Pol Pot's Favorite Bawdy Limericks

Who's on the Stand First? The Comedy Routines of Joe McCarthy and Roy Cohn

You're Putin Me On, or, Vlad All Over

About the author:

Marc Brel was born in a bunk. His mama died and his daddy got drunk. He never ever learned to read or write so well, but he could play a guitar just like ringin' a bell. When he was 17, it was a very good year for small-town girls and soft summer nights.

By falsely claiming on his college application to be Native American and president of his high school's chapter of Future College Benefactors of America, Brel gained admission to the very prestigious Washington University in St. Louis, but he got confused and ended up at the very obscure St. Louis University in Washington by mistake. There, he majored in Gastroenterology, because he thought it would be a gut. He dropped out after one semester and tried to enlist in the Marine Corps, but he got confused again and ended up in the Peace Corps.

The Peace Corps sent Brel to Uganda, which at the time was ruled by the infamous despot, Idi Amin. The entire world was horrified and appalled by the brutal, egomaniacal dictator, but Brel thought he was funny. That a dangerously incompetent, narcissistic sociopath with no discernible governing skills could become the leader of a country struck Brel as hilarious, and it became the theme of much of his work. The humorous essay he submitted to the Entebbe *News*, entitled, "Amin No Disrespect, but Idi Really Slays 'Em" was never published, but it did get him the hell out of Uganda.

Brel's first joke book, *The Grass is Always Greener Over the Mass Graves: The Wit of Joey Stalin* was nominated for a Pulitzer Prize, but failed to win because, regrettably, there is no Pulitzer Prize category for joke books, and self-nominations are not allowed. However, he has two National Book Awards. He got one on eBay, and the other at a pawn shop in Paramus, New Jersey.

The Trump Administration and Other Jokes is his eighth or ninth book, we've lost track. If it sells enough, he won't need to write another one. So please, buy this book.